W9-BJZ-765

TEACHERS Are Awesome!

ISBN: 978-1-68088-283-4

Printed in China.
First Printing: 2019

⊕ This book is printed on recycled paper.

This book is printed on paper that has been specially produced to be acid free (neutral pH) and contains no groundwood or unbleached pulp. It conforms with the requirements of the American National Standards Institute, Inc., so as to ensure that this book will last and be enjoyed by future generations.

Blue Mountain Arts, Inc.
P.O. Box 4549, Boulder, Colorado 80306

TEACHERS

Are Awesome!

written and illustrated by
ronnie walter

Blue Mountain Press™
Boulder, Colorado

There's a reason why we always remember our favorite teachers.

They celebrate your successes, support your ideas, and nudge you through the trickier parts of a lesson.

Teachers smile when you come into the classroom and don't let anyone get away with goofing off...

well, not too much anyway.

Teachers make a difference.

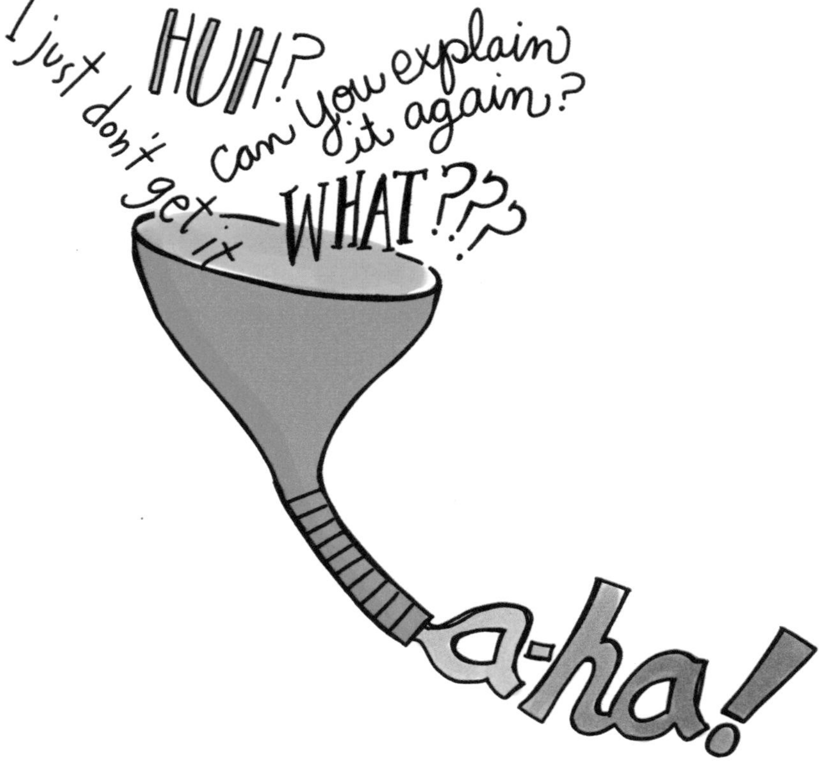
I just don't get it
HUH?
can you explain it again?
WHAT?!?
a-ha!

Teachers take complex ideas and make them easier to understand...

over and over and over!

They find just the right words to reach a student who is struggling...

or hurt...

or bored.

Teachers do more than just deliver information.

They...

They encourage you to keep doing your best every day.

Teachers are continuously looking for new ways to keep their lessons lively and engaging so their students grow and blossom.

They live for the sound of laughter in their classroom, the spark of passion in the eyes of their students, and all the little moments that truly matter.

But what makes a teacher really happy?

Hearing those three little words,

"I get it!"

Teachers care that their students are...

CAPABLE

curious

OPEN-MINDED

independent

& Loved.

Teachers accept that teaching is a full-time job with an added bonus of a part-time job to fill their evenings and weekends.

They know their world not only revolves around their students, but parents and administrators too.

But they keep refilling their toolboxes with...

discipline

Creativity

PATIENCE

ENTHUSIASM

ENERGY...

...and the largest cup of coffee they can find so they're ready for whatever comes next.

Teachers don't always feel like angels or saints or superheroes, but to their students, they are all those things—and more.

And you?

About the Author

From the first time she was handed a blank piece of paper and a crayon, Ronnie Walter knew what she wanted to do for a living—draw pictures and tell stories!

She has been a successful artist and writer for over twenty years, and her words and pictures have been used for books, fabrics, home accessories, gift items, greeting cards, and much more.

Ronnie lives in a little house by the water with her husband and their rescue Catahoula Leopard Hound, Larry.